Twenty Is Winter

I

Ahla Iqbal

Published by Ahla Iqbal, 2023.

TWENTY IS WINTER

First edition. September 2, 2023.

Copyright © 2023 Ahla Iqbal.

ISBN: 979-8223315056

Written by Ahla Iqbal.

Table of Contents

CHAPTER 1 | Introduction 1
CHAPTER 2 5
Chapter 3.. 11
Chapter 4.. 19
Chapter 5.. 23
Chapter 6.. 27
Chapter 7.. 35
Chapter 8.. 41
Chapter 9.. 51
Chapter 10... 55
Chapter 11... 59
Chapter 12... 63
Chapter 13... 67
Chapter 14... 71
Chapter 15... 77
Chapter 16... 81

To the heart that i would love to carry in my heart, my inspiration!

CHAPTER 1
Introduction

Winter had started a week before.. The swooshy sound of winds.., I could still hear them from inside. I took my side lazily cozying myself facing the woods that were under fire only to give us the warmth to survive. I watched those woods getting into ashes, ice crystals were falling so hard by then. For a moment it interrupted me, with a big noise. But I got back to them without much struggles. The snip-snap-whoosh of those woods were sizzling blaze, far enough to comfort me and my body. I kept my head down to watch them more closely. For a second, I was able to hear the sound of their last breath, I looked at them, now with my inner eyes to hear what they are trying to tell me. Then, they made me stuck in a thought, it was so sudden. For some moments, I mistook them as me.. A deep sigh. I couldn't even argue to myself that it was all a thought since my tears had jumped already from the strong bluish eyes that beholds many... "We have a similar life.." I thought. My mother by then had already made a coffee for me and she was drinking hers. I was then too reckless to drink it before it turns into an icy rock.

" What are you staring at, have your coffee" She murmured. My coldish hands longed, to unite with the hot coffee glass. I took them in an instant like it would be snatched by someone before me. What made me to think like this way? It has no answer....

My mother, by then was getting ready to go outside to collect some woods, every day we would go out and collect the woods. It would continue till the snow falling gets worse. We will be completely shut inside when the intensity of the weather gets so high. I longed to go outside at all the times, it needs a lot of efforts to survive the world outside the door. Today I took my favorite sweater to wear. It was a dark brown sweater with a cute tiny heart on the left bottom corner of the sweater. My coloured sweaters found its place in the corners. It was a deathly silenced world until I opened the door... The swooshy sounds of cold wind became much stronger than before. It marched in vigor into my ears. I was then so lazy and was in a state of mind to-not-to-put my foot outside the door, even though I had loved to go out. The wind was in a rush and rough, but it had a kind of rhythm of its own. Then, why was I not able to find the muse in them? Was it because of the way it came out to me..? "Girl, come fast, get away from your thoughts.." my mom murmured again. The snow in me got melted and I got back into my sense.. I walked so hard with my stick.. It then reminded me of my earlier days when I was a happy little child with many friends to play. As a child I was so thrilled to go outside with my mom to collect woods in winter, I would cry and beg to her to take me along, but she simply won't take me. By then, winter days were so much of fun, I could play and do anything inside my house, my only concern was to go out with mom to collect woods. Now, I could go with my mom to collect some woods, but it looks frustrating for me.. How brilliant is the play of time!

After all the hassles of collecting woods, I would spread a woolen mat besides the firewoods, then I would stack my pillows to read in comfort. Since it was comfortable more than enough, it makes me to fall in to a deep sleep without much efforts. Eyes would be widely open and curious to watch the dreams that gets enacted before me when I read a book. My life during winter was occupied with hot coffee, staring at the woods in fire, collecting woods, reading books and helping my mother. There would be no change and I wasn't able to make any changes to them. All my instincts have to wait till the winter is over. But, the winter is always long.

I always had a love for old belongings. I craved, day by day, to read some hand written letters. But, who is there to write! Even though, I was so cold inside, I too had a mind to love and waiting for the arrival of someone who could love me like the love of rain to the Earth. And its winter now, so nothing would come. Often, I found myself staring at the letterbox. It was kept unused for ages, the box is now rusty and is completely covered by snow. No one, including me doesn't care to tidy it up, thus we got no letters. That day I took a decision to keep it clean, to make it visible so we could get our letters... Just a hope made by my hopeful mind with a little hope.

"Give me an old kind of love and a box full of letters," every beats of my heart sang this song.. The beauty of its rhythm was glittering in my eyes. Its loveliness made its entrance upon my lips, with a soft smile, as the one who is completely maddened by her first love..

Slowly, I closed my eyes to welcome the awaiting sweet dreams to wither its poppy effects...

Being a child, I found myself, a happy soul at each passing seasons.

CHAPTER 2

A Long Winter

Now, it's not about a season, it's about me... Winter comes & then, it goes, sooner or later, the thing is that the winter in me was too lazy to vanish. I don't know how much time will it takes to welcome the summer.. A moody girl like me, with a brown-black eyes, only shines in brown when the sunlight falls on the eyes, but there is no sunshine strong enough to face those eyes and its grief's.....

I always thought if there is really someone in this world who is strong enough to face my eyes. I had met with many eyes and those were just an ordinary for me. The cupid was tired, and got failed in their attempts to find someone for me. I want to love, and I want to be loved, by the one I love. Nothing happened. The cupid took a break.

I always found myself in an agony, I couldn't make myself happy anymore like I did when I was a child. I wished for a great entry of someone into my life, to lighten up my world. We might at some point of life may need someone to help us to see how beautiful and valuable we were, we may need someone and their love for us to make us look back into us to realise the beauty that we holds. The reason for my agony, when looked carefully, might be the loneliness that made me and my happy soul buried in a great agony. I knew that the winter in me is a constant thing and I could do nothing to change it. But there is something that I could do. I could remove the winter around me that was staying for a long time. I remember that I had told you before about a letter box. It was now all cleaned up, now the letter box is what makes my home more scenic than before. But not quite sure about the arrival of its guest... Now that it was all cleaned up, I decided to open the room which was always closed, were all the old belongings and the memories were kept, one thing that I have to say is that those aren't mine. The room was completely in a mess. It wore a dress made up of spider's net, just like my mind. Everything in it was so cold and dusty.. Took some days to make it completely clean... There must be a lot of things that is mysterious, beautiful and treasurable, I thought...

Even though, I wasn't carrying much energy emotionally to do something newer and fresher, I was trying, just trying to find a way to get me out of this cobweb of hardships.. I looked into every nook and corner of that mysterious room... When I was at a time, a happy soul, this mysterious door and room was out of my sight, I had never seen it before or cared.. But now, it came just in front of me like a ghost friend to whom I gave a helping hand to get out from the bottle and is now willing to do or give me anything that I wishes for.. It must be because of the idle soul in me.. Yes, I too think so, of the old saying that everything around you will be visible to you only when you don't possess anything greater than those.. Anyway, it just appeared out of now where. An ordinary room to a mysterious and a beautiful room.

Suddenly, after looking over the inside part of the room in a blink of an eye, it took my sight, an old box. It was made out of woods. Wait.. there is something, really.. What's that? A cassette it seems.. I took them, and went into my room in a hurry.. Took my radio and put those cassettes in it carefully.. The curiosity in me was boiling till it got played.

A scratch..

How old would that be? No idea, it wasn't playing.. I'm now, really, so horribly depressed for this.. It looks like I lost something from my hand that was kept tightly..

Seconds, minutes and hours had passed. The bed is now ready to welcome the soothing sleep.. Somehow, I pulled myself to sleep... My eyes were carrying much weight like my heart does. I took my side facing the glass window witnessing the fall of snow, how romantic it is, I thought. My hands cuddled tightly to feel the feel of love, the divine feel, a soothing world.. I got melted into the very moment..

A voice was spread, interrupting that moment.. It came to me like an embrace, an embrace to the loneliness I felt at that moment.. Those cassettes were now working!

" To my rooh, let me spread my pinching soul,
when we meet, when our eyes could meet,
let me taste thy soul from your lips..
Soon, our hands could meet, I hope so...
When i'm tied to you, with the red thread of fate, we will cherish,
Thy love, our love and my love.."

A pause.. a long pause.. for me to digest what I heard!

I stood up and sat besides the window to feel the world of love.. A seed of love then sprouted in me amidst the snow in me.. I wanted to hear the rest of the cassettes, but for today I don't have the ability to hold the power of love. This one had already made a poppy effect.. Slowly.. I would hear them all.. I want to hear them, the love, slowly, by cherishing the love.. That feeling itself is making my whole body shiver, and that too was, I can't explain!

I had a soulful sleep, the voice was continuously played in my dream and I smiled like an idiot who just fell in love.

The morning came, the firewoods were burning, but it was left unnoticed. For all my attention was in those cassettes. I was curious enough to know the owner of the voice, I was wondering why the cassettes are at my home and who send that here? There is a mysterious-love part that was left hidden for a very very long time. Okay, it will be unwired slowly. I hurried and rushed to hear the rest. My heart was beating so hardly, it looks like those were sent to me by my lover... Ha ha, an impossible thing... How can a love change someone? I had wondered about the same. Now I knows. Even a love story that's about to unfurl is making me so mad in the feel of love.

".. it's raining, & the winds are whispering thy love,

my body, it's

aching, to hug you till my clothes

takes away all your fragrances,

pour your love upon me, i'm craving

to be soaked in your love.."

Oh my God, I can't withstand this... It is so beautiful to watch two souls falling in love, the way they love and the language of their love...

I was wondering if there are love like this in this world. Is it really for someone from my own house? Is it my mom's! No, no way.. Aww, god i'm so curious and too happy to find more about this... I too want to fall in love, I want to feel the feel of love.. I wish to be treasured, soothed, touched, and loved... Why am I a soul with such a fate?

My heart was beating so loudly, when I dreamed about the kind of love I would have and the voice I heard from the cassettes and their love. I feared that my mom would find this secret of mine. At some times, i smiled so lovely, it was really the smile of love, the one who is in love or was in could realise so easily that i'm being affected by love.. This lovey girl tried so hard to hide her soft smile from the mother.. There was a problem, the cassettes, the rest of the cassettes were completely scratched.. Oh, I am so down, at least let me fall in love by hearing an old love story..

The snow began to melt..

The spring had marked its arrival..

And this lady in love was waiting for the snow to fade, to clean out the scratches of the cassettes.. A curious mind it was...

Chapter 3

An Encounter

03-01-1992.

A lovely day it was.. For some days, I was not the old me.. I felt really a good change in me. I chose this very day to go out, all alone, just to be alone, to embrace the happiness in loneliness. With all the feelings that I got from the lovely-voices, I hoped to be indulged in the ocean of thoughts of love. That day I chose to walk, then to take a bus. But as I walked, my inner thoughts asked me to just walk, the winds came to hold my hands and gave a breeze on my hair... And kissed me like a lover.

I don't quite remember the situation that got me into this man! It all happened at an instant. I was totally flabbergasted! Let me narrate what happened with the pieces of memory that is still left in me. That moment totally buried me somewhere, like I was transported to an other world.There are some kind of memories that we can't narrate completely. Standing upon this world, I won't be able to narrate and let you understand what it feels to be taken into an other world, that doesn't even exists. But only do I know that they exists. Never ever in my life, I had this kind of an ' eye contact'! Do you know that, how beautiful is an eye contact? The world around me was totally blurred at that moment. At first it made me uncomfortable for looking into my eyes in such a way, without even blinking, i was not nervous, but more than that. Not an ordinary eye, it seems. I have a thought that we both felt the same.. Really, i'm not lying.. There were no words or any other things, but only that very 'eye contact moment', we walked away when we got hit by the reality.. At that time, it was just like, meeting a beautiful person in a journey. A single portrait or just a glimpse that will never come again, I thought so. At that moment, I got to knew the power of an eye contact... Eyes are connected, they are the lovers in disguise, when they meet the not- an ordinary one they stares at each other, because they knows everything about the love story that's about to happen by just a single stare.

I rushed to my home after relieving from the frozen moment that I had before and, after some time I took the radio and cassettes and went to the valley to lay upon the hills, thereby I could look at the sky, feel the greenness of the soil and the 'Love' at the same time... This girl is now really in a world of fantasy. She really don't have an idea why she was so happy, why she was smiling a lot, she was just happy without much reasons.. The cold breeze was so appealing to my soul, the fresh breathe after a very long time, the winds passed through my body by giving a chill... I spread myself over the green grasses of the hill... Placed my radio besides me, inserted the next cassette, tapped gently on the switches to play. Closed my eyes to witness the moment, the embracing moment... Let me tell you a secret, come closer, a little more, " i secretly went out on one day to fix those cassettes, without telling my mom".

" I do remember, still & always, the moment our eyes had met..

They were already kissing and blushing, the eyes.

Seconds & minutes & hours passed, the image was so vivid and vibrant.

I want to welcome every day and nights with the meeting of our eyes..

When will we meet? When will our eyes be able to console

each other for this long departure.."

Wait, Why do I get a feel that someone is talking about me? All these lines were picturising in my heart the man I met on that day.. It felt like these were his own words... You got the feel? Everything is just marking its arrival to let me remember him and his eyes...

At this moment, the clouds were so aesthetically dull... It seems like it will rain. A lovely breeze then came and gave me a cold chill over my body.. I got up and took everything and hurried to find a shelter. After all the feel was good, but I can't afford myself to devour the rain.. She just hoped to feel the feeling...It started pouring... The drops were dancing so gorgeously, a dreamy look, a perfect environment to read a book.. There was something that I forgot to tell you. I had got a letter, a very old letter from one of the covers of the cassettes. I took that to read.

Dear,

Writing from my heart to the one who lives in it..

Your lover is wailing for he doesn't have an idea about what we would become.. The most beautiful things that's lovable are always kept afar, this world is really envious of seeing the loving souls together.. Thus, i'm confused about our future. Then there is our love, that doesn't fluctuates or have any access to outsiders. This love shall remain the same. I will write many letters for you, and also I would do the same thing that we were doing till now. This man will share his love to you through the 'love letter' program in the radio, to make this world, the hearers, the witness of our love... Like the poetry, that remains for all the time, I wish to make our love story to transcend to all the ages, to be read.. I don't want our love to be vanished after our lives. Let it be known to the world, after we are vanished from this world. I'm weary of this world.. When can I meet you, my beautiful lady? Where can I wait for you? Write to me, i'm wailing to read your words.."

So these are the letters that are sent to the above mentioned show, to be read.. This might have been a long distance relationship. It seems like they have been connecting each other daily, even at a long distance! A kind of love, so pure and wild and exquisite!

Want to know more and more about this love and its story... Their love must be known to everyone like what they had wished before... I would be so happy to be a part of this..

The rain had marked its departure, the smell of the soil after rain, was released into the nature. The beauty of nature is rather supreme.. I walked to the direction of my home, my long white dress were touching the earth below like waving a goodbye to them, giving a promise to meet them again... When I reached home, my mind was forcing me to ask my mom more about those cassettes, but I was too shy... After gathering some confidence, I asked her about the cassettes. She told me that she had no idea about anything that was there in the room. Everything belonged to her mom and no one had dared to touched them. So this might be my grandma's precious belongings... I never had an idea of my grandma's this part of love... A beautiful love story, she was having, but wasn't known to anyone from her family, but what about the end. Did they end up being together? How could I get to know more about this? With time, it would come, I swear.

A day of coincidences and surprises, I was totally astonished. Those eyes weren't ready to bid farewell to my mind. I think it got stuck in me. Am I in love? I don't know it yet, what it feels to love someone... It was something that I was longing to experience. May be, I would be able to have it soon. Those coincidences and fate, are they really true? When will we meet? Will there be an another chance or not? Let's see, I thought. I met him a lot in my dreams, we talked and became really good friends. Those dreams passed on to me a kind of feeling that it's all true. I started to like him through my dreams. Then, I fell in love with him. It was so good to love someone through the sequences of dreams. Since, the reality was so cruel, I hoped to live in a dreamy life. A mad woman is she! A woman who's madly in love with a stranger, but I told you before that their eyes were not a stranger, they were lovers in the past. I hoped for the coincidences, everyday.

But, there were no such coincidence or meetings like I wished. Days, weeks and months passed, not even a trace of him was there. It took me more time than enough to realise my feelings for him. It was growing with the days passing. Those eyes really had an impact upon me. Does it looks inappropriate to you? It might seems so, but that was the reality... I may have witnessed many eyes and souls for many a times, but they were not even able to have an impact upon me like those eyes of that man that I met earlier... It came straight into my soul to mark its existence. I became so sad for the fate of not being able to spot him again... Even the nature was having the same emotion like me, but was not ready to lend me a helping hand. One should seek their love by their own.

"Don't let my hands go idle, I whispered in shiver. Give me an old kind of love, I whispered again. But, you were gone so far away from me..." my heart complained.

But there was an unsure thought upon my feelings for him. For I didn't knew the reason for me falling for him so soon. We were a total strangers, so how could I love someone who is so strange to me. But I think that's the beauty of love and that's why we are trembling to define what love is. Now, I remember an old grandma, who once told me about love when I asked her what it is.

She told me, " Little girl, there's no well-suited definition for a love, that I could find, you would feel it when you grow up".

Now, I know what she meant!

Chapter 4

The Second Encounter

08-08-1992

I went to a market with my mom. After purchasing, I told my mom that I would go home later. At that time, I wished to spend some more time outside. Decided to visit a library nearby. Sat there for some time, read a book and went to sit at the sea-side benches. There was a soothing wind, I was enjoying it a lot. I closed my eyes just for a moment to feel it as a whole. To my surprise when I opened my eyes, I felt a presence, of someone sitting beside me. A man was sitting beside me wearing a black coloured shirt. His hair was swinging along with the wind, it gave me a feel that I had met him before. But I didn't had the courage to look at him for more time.

"What he would think of me?" I thought.

I was just curious to know if we had studied together, but he might not be thinking the same as me. I took my eyes off him and started to focus on myself. Soon, I did felt a presence of eyes looking at me, I turned my head to look and I saw that man looking at me. That's him! I would never forget his eyes! But why he is here, sitting besides me and looking at me? I didn't had any idea. At that time I was in doubt, and I didn't had any idea about him appearing infront of me. I let it slide off. This lady was not ready to get her into a world of love without having his approval, I just wished to not to hurt myself. May be he might not be having the same thought as mine. At that time, I was having this skill to hide what my heart was feeling. He took his departure after some time. I happened to notice a book just after his departure, he had left there a book. Had a sight over the book, Oh God, it's the same book that I had read an hour before in the library. My mind without thinking much asked me to call that man, to stop him and to give his book back. When I showed him the book, he looked at me and left after a smile. Then, I had no way but to keep that book in my bag and then, i went straight to my home. I can't just leave that book alone.

I was smiling inside, how come he's here, with me.. Oh God, what does that mean? A coincidence! May be it is.. I headed to my home. On my way back, I was thinking about the second encounter. I don't know why i'm feeling like this. Anyway, it's so good to have a happy and smiling heart...

"To my heart, I am asking you, don't overthink".

I felt, at each encounters, a change in me, a slow process it was but had a great impact on me and was fixed, there was no going back to the older self, a different person, I became by each passing days. I don't know why he is doing this and why i'm, too. Maybe it's just my inner thought or a misunderstanding. Falling in love isn't simple, we need to think and think and think. At first, I need to know more about him and let him to know more about me. Before that, I need to draw a clear portrait of my feelings towards him. I need to be sure about my feelings. What if all these thoughts gets faded away in a moment.

Those eyes, for sure, was trying to tell me something. It gave me butterflies in my stomach. The thing was constantly played upon my head. On each days, these thoughts came without a knock. Whenever I think of something, he comes directly into me.

"Oh, God I can't escape from him".

At that moment, I was actually trying to remove him from my thoughts. I don't want to make me fall for him so soon, I was afraid that I would hurt myself.

Chapter 5

A New Winter

The summer was over, and the winter came there to mark its arrival.. Winter is here, again and not exactly like it was before. A slight change, I could feel that. Not that intense, but there's a change for sure. I found a better me taking birth by each passing seasons. Now, the firewoods are no longer having my attention. Many days had passed, even months. You had missed a great part of me.

" It's hard to fake feelings through the eyes", I think so. And they knows who their partner will be in the future, I had mentioned this earlier. 'Love vision of eyes', let me call it like this. Do you know about this legend of 'Love vision of eyes'? Let me narrate... Our eyes, they aren't just eyes, they have a vision, a love vision, to recognise its partner. It means that our eyes could tell us with whom we would end up together in the future. That's why the eye contacts are so intense. Sometimes, we may not recognise what our eyes are trying to tell us. So, believe in your eyes, it won't lie. And I need to believe in my eyes. I hoped to. And then what, I grew becoming fonder of him.

When the seasons were changing, my feelings and thoughts too were doing the same. He lived in the castle, in my heart. I can't explain or convey to you about how it became like this. How he became a part of mine? I don't know, but I now have a feeling towards him. And I'm quite sure about this feeling. It's love, I knew it. Before the arrival of winter itself, I was in love, a single sided love it was. The cool breeze of the winter came and was embracing me by then, like a man. My hairs were flipping and dancing in the air. The lips, they were so red and the cheeks were blushing. My eyes were shining so brightly because the renter is him. My mom asked me, "Your eyes are shining so beautifully than before". And I blushed again with a sweet smile. He came into my world and lightened them with his eyes.

It was so long since I had played those cassettes. I rushed to the balcony of my room to play the cassettes.

"It's falling snow outside and a beautiful love story is playing in the balcony of my home and an exquisite man is living in my mind".

You could imagine the feeling. It's something like, a special kind of feeling. It can only be felt. The snow was falling inside my heart too, giving my heartbeats a rhythm, a rhythm of love.

Took the cassettes out and played it,

"... I wish if you were here by my side, when it snows to give me the warmth, can't we meet? I can't wait darling, I would run breathtakingly, only to hold you in my arms, to hold your hip, then, to dance slowly in the rain, i'd then lean towards you to hold you closer. Till you come here, i'll wait or else I'd run there to take you home, to adorn the freshness of summer nothing could stop us my darling..."

I thought, that would be enough for today. While I was listening to these romantic voices it was him who came into my mind. It felt every time like that's his voice. I realised that I fell for him. But the process, I don't know. I don't know how things came to be like this. The only thing that I'm aware of is that I love him. No wonder, love is really inexplicable. I don't know, when those eyes stamped love for him in my heart. The time is really magical!

A love, without a hope of a return, was the kind of love I had. It was always impossible to have. But it was growing so hardly. I don't think that I could find any words in this world to explain how I feel about him. I just wanted him to love me, I just want him. Even if he can't stand by himself, I could be his walking stick, and my love would be still the same. I won't let another woman to have him, so I decided to pursue him, since I can't withstand the thought of losing him to other woman.

Chapter 6

My Existence!

To mark my existence, I went out. The snow wasn't that worse, so I didn't backed up. At first, he should know that I exist in this world. Went to the same library that I visited last time. Took a book, just to confuse the people out there. My eyes were already searching for him. He wasn't there. After some thoughts, I went to sit on the same bench near the beach. It was so cold, but it couldn't bother me, I was so determined. I closed my eyes for a second, like I did the last time. And opened it with a hope-filled smile. Searched for him, my mind already started to imagine that he was sitting beside me smiling at me and holding a book. Imagination just stood as it was like. He wasn't there. I was totally devastated. Decided to have a walk over the beach. After some times, I walked to the bus station, to get into the bus. It was a bus to my home and it will not be that good to make my journey late, it might snow hardly at night... Looks like the bus was about to go. I ran fastly to get into it. Within some time, I managed to get into it. Then there came a man recklessly towards the door and we got hit together. At that time, I was like, What the hell is this, can't he be...

"Sorry, I didn't meant to…" He said.

I looked at him. It was him, the one who I love.

I said " It's you?", the funniest part is that I said it so loudly.

"Do I know you?" He asked.

"Oh God, what's more embarrassing…" I thought.

I said, " Nothing, please move aside". Since, it was cold, I rubbed my hands together to hide my embarrassing mind.

He gave the way and I went straight into the bus and found myself a seat and sat there like nothing had happened. And that bus, it wasn't at all ready to go. It waited there for ten more minutes for other passengers. The seats were now almost filled. There was only me in my seat. And I was sitting almost at the back of the bus. Now, the bus was about to start and there came the last passenger. And that too was him… At that point of time, I wasn't ready to meet him for the second time. I saw him walking towards me. With each steps of him, my heart beats were so rapidly intense.

"Do you mind me sitting here?" He asked.

I replied, " No, you can". While saying this my body and even my cheeks were vibrating. I tried my best to hide it, and my laugh I used to wear upon my face to cover them was too embarrassing…. I sat there like a statue, felt so embarrassed. He offered me a hot tea. I thanked him and took a sip without much thinking. It gave me some warmth. "He is so considerate".

I stood up when the bus stopped at my destination leaving on my seat, that book, that was left by him, on that day. He might have seen that. The chances are less for him to remember me. From his behaviour, I don't think that he has that kind of feeling towards me like I had for him.

"So, I need to work harder", I thought.

On my way back, while walking, I was thinking about him. I didn't had any idea about what to do to make him fall for me. That incident of book is really a mystery, I don't know why he did like that. It might be just my misunderstanding. I got depressed at this thought. I was so madly in love with him, by then.

Oh, I forgot to explain how he looks. In my eyes, he seems to be the perfect and the handsomest man on this earth. He is 5'6", looks like he's doing some workouts. I can see that his features are getting an upgradation. He have a dark brown eyes with great sunshine falling upon them, it was sparkling whenever I looked at them. About his smile, a catching and a breathtaking one it is, at each moments when he smile, I fell much harder for him. Looks like the whole world is moving me towards him to hug him. A silent soul is he, when he gets outside, I think so. I really do love that kind of man. A man who is so calm and generous to the people outside. I guess he might be so cheerful and talkative to his closest ones. What I love the most about him is his hair. When his hair falls upon his forehead, I can't breathe, at that moment, he becomes more than handsome. I know that many girls like the boys with beards and moustaches. But, for me his clean- shaved look is the favourite one! Oh god, when he smiles, It feels like I would fall down because of the hotness that he spreads around him.

I was deeply thinking about the way that I should use to approach him to let him notice me and my existence. I don't want to make him think that I'm a creepy creature, stalking him like other girls, but as the one who should be treasured. I was thinking about all the possible ways even while, I was watching a movie. It was snowing outside and it might get worst by days passing. So it will not be possible for me to go out. Everyday, I should be at my home. In the midst of the ocean of my thoughts, one of the scenes of the movie got my attention. The heroine in that movie, was also deeply enchanted by a man like me. She chose to write a sequence of love letters, that narrates a tale of her and love story, with him as the hero. Her plan was to use those to confess to him. In that way, he would be able to catch all her feelings easily without losing the genuinity.

There are chances that he would think of this woman, me as the rest of his admirers. He might not notice my genuinity. He should feel that. She should be different in his eyes, not like the rest . But, a very special one. In this era, the one who cares to pursue his/her love even if it seems impossible must be only out of intense love, a love that is so rare. Even though, it all seems impossible, with some efforts those could be made possible. Seeking the impossible is what makes our life a adventurous one. For me, his love looks impossible. But, I am ready to face those impossible wall between us, I could break them. The fixed notion of impossibility that distances the pure love.

On one night, I played those cassettes again and again, to hear the rest, to find more about them and their love story, what if I could create a beautiful love story like them, I thought. Their love story was incomplete and I wondered if I could get the rest of their story, I thought again. I asked my mother about her mother's marriage and all those things. But I found nothing related to the part of love story that I heard, I witnessed them all alone. There was a name on the postcard, and it wasn't my grandpa's. Then, I knew that the hero of my grandma was someone else. I asked my mother if her mom had at once told her anything about her love. She told me that, at some points, she had found her mother sitting idly and reading something. The tears would be then flowing like in a river. I asked her if she had seen what was inside those letters.

" Your grandma never allowed us to enter that room, so how can i?"

" and we hadn't thought that hard, and we never had asked her the reason..." my mother told.

"But she loved all her children and the father of her children, she was tasting all the pains alone, we, her kids, were not mature by then to realise, if she was here, I would run to her and would give her a tight hug, I want to tell her that she is not alone, we all are here for you..." My mom was crying.

So, she might have had a bad ending for her love story, I thought. Once again, in entered that old room. But, I think that there is no end for a love story, it would continue to live in them till they die. I searched the whole room again and again and again. Hoped to rediscover something new. I felt something was igniting in me. My eyes caught a small portrait that was there lying at one of the corners of the room. I took them carefully by my hands. It was my grandma's. And there was a man beside her and he was not my grandpa, it should be that man, her lover, the one sent her the love notes. Ok, but where can I find more about him. I decided to keep that portrait in my wooden box. May be, it would help me in the future, I thought. This might be a great help for me to find more about their story.

After this, my grandma's love story was almost over, nothing was found later. It remained as an unfinished love. But it transcended over time, without vanishing, for they left the world with their love. My grandmas love story gave me a kind of strong feeling that I should never make a reason to lose my love, otherwise, I too would become like her. I want to find a solace for her, I wish to find her a solace in her grand child's love.

Chapter 7

Snow Camp

A situation occurred, the snow became worse. And we were asked to move away from our houses. We took our necessary things and belongings and went to a camp nearby the town. A jeep came over there at our place and we all got our things and ourselves into that jeep. After some time, they started the jeep, and we got farther away from our houses. I looked at them with a a hope to return. From a distance, I barely saw the camp. A golden light was brimming upon the white coat. When I reached there, there wasn't that many peoples, there were only a few people like us. We got our part and we placed all our things there, I was quite satisfied with the portion that I got for myself. The mothers over there ganged up and started talking about the snow and other things. The children started playing their usual games, and the old souls too gathered together and was talking and laughing. I was so happy to see many happy souls out there. Looked like a family gathering after a very long time. I smiled with all my heart. Then, I decided to get busy with my hobby, I took my book, pen and my radio and the wooden box with me. And I sat outside, at a little distance from the camp. I already had became adjusted with the snow and coldness. The love in me was such a warmth. A thought of him could give me the warmth that I need. I was so obsessed and determined to pursue him. I wrote some poems, some love poems, thinking about him. Then I closed my eyes and dreamed about him. After some time, I came back from my sleep hearing a sound of a man. It was so similar. He was walking towards me and was getting closer and closer. I looked at him to see his face, at first it was not clear. His face became clearer as he approached me and then I recognised him. Your guess is right, it's him! He came there with a smile over his face and asked,

"Why are you sitting here, all alone?"

I replied, " I was just sitting, to pass the time".

Him: "It looks like you were writing something".

Me: "Yes, I was writing, writing some poems".

Him: "Oh, you write poems? That's amazing!"

Me: " Thank you, so kind of you".

Him: "You seemed familiar to me, that's why I came here".

Me: "We had met at the bus station and you had offered me a tea"

Oh God, what am I doing, things are getting more embarrassed, what in the world has happened to me, I murmured to myself.

Him: " Oh, that's it. If you don't mind can I read your poems?"

Me: "Oh, sure, you can, it's my pleasure".

I directed the book to him and he started reading my poems. I was so shy since they were the romantic poems and that too about him.

"Here, your book. Your poems, they are really good. You do have a skill!"

He told.

"Do you write poems every day?" He added.

Yes, most of the times, it gives me a great feeling", I replied.

"I'll let you write, don't want to spoil your mood, I'll take my leave, you may continue", he said and he walked away after giving me a soft and cute smile.

I was sitting there like a frozen statue. All these were unexpected, i never thought that we would meet so soon. So, there are more chances for us to meet again. Now, I started to love the camp more than before. I was dancing inside my mind for meeting him again...

After some time, I went inside, I sat beside my mom and the rest. There I saw him again. He was helping other men over there to give foods. He was so cool and kind. I found him laughing and being friendly with everyone over there. While I was staring at him doing all these things, he looked instantly at me. He caught me looking at him red handed. I smiled and he too did. He asked me to join him. He looked like a refreshing soul. An enchanting happiness was spread all over him. I slowly joined him and helped him. I thought that I would then be able to create a friendship with him. He then told everyone out there about my poems and me. But just like a good friend. We together did most of the jobs over there. There were many moments when we had accidentally got an eye contact. The air over there was filled with love and joy. It was so good over there than being alone at my home. Along with him, there was his best friend. He introduced me to him and we started to set up the sleeping room for old ones. It was both a joy filled and a happiest moment. We really had enjoyed those moments. He was talking and laughing a lot with his best friend. They were so bonded together. And it was an exquisite bond, I admired their bond. I felt so happy to be a part of them. I found a great change in him, when someone seriously asks him about something. Like I thought, he is so mature. He is talkative and closest to his dearest ones. He behaves carefully to the outsiders. It made me to fall for him more and more. At that moment, I knew that, he will never ever make me sad, if we get together, he is such a beautiful and a kind soul, I don't know anything about him other than these. But, I'm sure that he's a good one. So, I fell harder! For someone like me, he is the perfect one.

I took my leave when my mother called. He nodded his head with a smile. I went like a bird flying out of happiness. At that time, I was so happy...

The next day, when I came out, I saw him again laughing and talking and doing some chores with his best friend. They were so fine. Then they two went inside. I followed them and stared at him doing his jobs, i got caught by him standing there and staring at him. He waved at me and asked me to join them. I went when he called me again and again. It was just, I was so shy for getting caught many a times, but deep inside I wished to be with him. We all together sat on a bench and had our breakfast together. At that time, he talked to me and and it was a great feeling for me to have a conversation with him.. His vibe was just lit! A friendly soul is he. Soon, we became good friends. We all enjoyed our own company. I wished for the winter to last more. I remembered my last winter.

Chapter 8

First Kiss

We two became really good friends. We became so closer than before. More like a best friend. One night, we decided to take a walk outside. We talked while we were walking. There, I saw an old library. I asked him,

"Is it possible for us to get inside that library?"

"Yes, it is, I have the spare key with me, wait a while for me to return with key", he replied.

I was so excited. And waited for him. He came running and took hold of my right hand and ran towards the library. I got stuck. It gave me chills over my soul. He then, opened the library for me and asked,

"Are you happy?"

I nodded as a yes!

We then got inside of the library. There was some cobwebs and pigeons and some other things. And there were some snows too. He lighted a torch. The library was so beautiful to watch in the night time. Everything inside it was glittering in gold when the light fell over them. A nice moment it was. It might be because of his presence that I felt like this. When my eyes got stuck on a book upon one of the shelves, I took that to read. When I was looking over the pages, I saw him running towards me with something in his hands, to show me. The next moment, he was above me, and i don't remember how he fell into me, our lips, eyes, and everything was facing each other with a small distance between them, a little distance it was. My heart then began to beat so rapidly. I became breathless. I closed my lips tightier. There was a complete silence. I could hear him breathing. Our eyes were not at all blinking, they were staring at each other. I felt him becoming breathless, he too was feeling the same like me, I felt that. Everything was dark over there, only a small torch light was there. And we were alone. How romantic it was! The torch light reflected our faces and the details of our faces were so obvious. The golden light that fell upon our face made us to look beautiful. I saw a lovely smile spreading over him. I saw him moving closer towards me, there was no gap between us, now. The environment over there by then was so convenient to have a kiss. My heartbeats got doubled more than before. He was approaching me, finally his hands got hold of my hips. He leaned towards me. He kissed me soon after the torch lights stopped its lighting. It was all dark over then, everyone were in a deep sleep and there were only we two, kissing behind the darkness in the library. I then, smiled and took his hands over me, to interrupt the embarrassment and I moved back. We both then got back into the reality and decided to get back into our camp. He locked the library and we went out. On our way back, we talked about nothing. Everything was told from our silences. He then nodded at me and I too did and got back into our own rooms. I walked fastly and spread myself over my bed and closed my eyes. The moment came up by then, when I closed my eyes. Shyness blushed over my face and I took a side watching the night sky and redreamed about our moment. I was smiling so madly... Slowly, I got into a deep sleep.

The next morning, we both were feeling some kind of embarrassment at first. But it was all gone, after some time, when his best friend came there. We two were acting like nothing had happened before. It was so painful for me to act like there was nothing in my mind. But after that night, I felt much closer to him. I don't know what's going with him. And I was afraid, what if all those were just a dream, am I overthinking, I thought. I can't talk to him about this matter, and if I did what should I talk about? There came, after some days, a news update that, the snow would end soon. So, we may have to move back to our home in a very few days. I really didn't wanted to let the clock move its needles. My heart wished to have the skill to freeze the time.

The life at the camp was so refreshing, the people over there were so lovely. And he too was there, even though he wasn't one of the campers. He came there as one of the helpers. I got a lot of really nice friends and my mom too got many friends from there. Most of the mothers over there was of my mothers age. So, it was so easy for them to form a gang. I woke up early in the morning, like everyday. The morning breeze was so good over there. The snowing wasn't that worse compared to our place. It was beautiful and a whole new kind of experience I was having over there.

Thinking of going back to home itself was making me sad. He came to me when he found me sitting alone. He asked me what's bothering me. I said that it's nothing, but just mood swings. He then asked me to accompany them, when my mood becomes better. I went along with him at that moment itself and told him that I'm okay. We then got into our usual activities and had a long and meaningful conversations. He talked more about his life and dreams. I heard him so eagerly and patiently, for I was that much interested to know more about him by then and still now. He asked me about our returning date and all those things. I told him that I don't have any idea, it might happen suddenly, for I'm not sure about the weather and all those things.

Still, I was wondering inside, just by thinking about what all had happened till now. I had not expected that my life would become like this, one day. And I never ever in my life had expected that we would become this much closer. It's still a wonder to me and I really, I can't believe it.

On one fine morning, I was sitting on an arm chair, it was early in the morning. We could barely see the golden lights marking its arrival. When the light passes through the snow, the vision that we get is something, something that is so loving. And from that beautiful occurrence came he, he came out like a sparkling moon. I was gazing and became breathless. He was so handsome, my eyes were not at all ready to take their gaze from him. It looked like my dream prince coming from a white sky spreading sparkles of gold... I don't know how I controlled myself at that moment, without showing my love for him. My mind was asking me to run towards him to give him a tight hug.

And him, he had become a lover of my poems. He would ask me every time if I had wrote anything new. I started writing more poems daily than before, for him, to read. My writing skills too had updated over time. And my life too. After his arrival. He always told me to write more and gave me enough supports. On one Friday, we went out again, to a shop nearby, to buy some necessary things to the camp. It was such a lovely moment with him. We laughed and laughed and laughed. The shop wasn't opened, so we just waited there for it to be opened. We stood there and talked. We were standing so closely, and our hands were touching each other. At an instant, we became silent. A kind of feel was spread, something that arises when a boy and a girl gets closer. We looked at each other and stared. The air blew a warmth of love that went through our hairs, body and our souls. The shopkeeper made his arrival suddenly and interrupted, so we got back into our normal conversation like nothing had happened. After buying the necessary things, we went back to our camp. I don't know if he loves me or not. We two didn't had that courage to ask each other about our feelings. And I wasn't able to figure out his mind from his behaviour. I thought that, our process of falling in love is too much slower than a slow process, but we are enjoying the process. Even after all this, I'm not sure about we getting along. What will happen in the future is in the hands of the future itself. The time will reveal everything. We can't tell that.

Everyday, I felt that the camp was completely filled with happiness and love and care. Even though, it was snowing outside, our hearts were melting inside.

One day, I was busy in writing poems. And it was about him. I was blushing, while writing the poems. He came regularly knocking the door of my heart while I was writing. The breathless situation and the cheeks getting blushed while writing about him was really charming. When the ice was falling outside, I too was falling for him harder than them.

"What if I could hug you,

till my cloth takes away your

fragrance

for me to survive

the rest of

the lives."

I don't know from where he came, he came out of nowhere and hid behind me. When I saw him I closed my book. He got that I was writing something, and he knew those were poems. Then, he snatched it from me. I was so shy to let him read because I was writing about him. With his thought, I was writing those lines. He might not know, but I knew. I felt so embarrassed to face him. And again my face started to blush. He read it so loudly. I was able to feel the wavering in his voice, he looked at me and read such kind of poems I wrote before in that book. He closed the book and came towards my direction slowly. With each steps, my heart beated loudly. He then came closer and closer and closer and leaned towards me. Kept one of his hands on the top of the chair near to my head and the other hand on one of the hands of the chair. He pushed the chair backwards and leaned towards me. I became so nervous and I tried my level best to hide my nervousness. He wasn't stopping. He leaned more closer to me. And moved his sharp eyes to mine. And smiled. He was so handsome when he smiled. My hairs started to move along with his breath. Then, he pulled the chair and took his hands off and smiled at me for one more time. I was so freezed at that moment. He asked,

"Did I make you nervous?"

"Eh, no, I'm not nervous", I replied hiding my nervousness.

He laughed and said, "Okay" and blinked at me.

"I was just joking, you may continue your writing", he added.

He went after saying this. I took my book and stood up and took a nice breath and ran without any break towards my room over there. For my luck, he didn't caught me running like that.

The day arrived. Now it's time for us to return to our houses. He helped me get everything ready. I haven't noticed any sadness upon his face. Hardly, I was covering my sadness over a fake smile. I thought that he would say something before I take my departure from there. My heart was crying with the thought of leaving him, those days were so beautiful. It was really after a very long time, that I had smiled from my heart. It felt like a rediscovery of my older self, when I was a happy little soul. I was enjoying it. The time was flying so fastly. While I walked towards the car, a thread, an invisible one was holding me back. I took small steps, but the way was so small. We all said our goodbyes to everyone out there. And I personally went towards him and told,

"Then... I will be going now..."

I wanted to say a lot of things but I wasn't able to do that.

I was already talking a lot to him with my eyes.

He replied, " Ok then, let's meet again, be safe".

He then hugged me and I went straightly into our car without looking at anyone and straightly got into it. The car accelerated, I looked back to see him, I saw him standing there, happily waving at me.

I leaned my head over the window and closed my eyes to stamp his face on my heart. My eyes were crying by then.

Chapter 9

At Home

After returning from the camp, I was totally having less amount of energy. I missed him at every seconds and minutes and hours. My love for him got intensified more than before. Now, I'm madly in love with him. But I won't make any move recklessly. I wish to give him some time to fall in love with me. I do have more interest in the slow process of falling in love. I want to cherish all those moments.

One day, on one fine morning, I decided to visit the library that we had been to at that night. I took out the cassettes with me. Went there with a hope that we would meet. Walked to the bus station and took the bus to my destination with much hope and enthusiasm. When the stop was approaching, I felt an increased beating of my beats in my heart. And the bus stopped, I got out of it. I felt that the world around me was revolving at a higher speed. My eyes were searching for him, already. I took my footsteps to the direction of the camp. I was sure that he wouldn't overthink about my visit as we were so close. When I reached there, the first person I saw there was him. He too came there for a visit like me. What a coincidence! I ran towards him and gave him a shake hand. I asked him to accompany me to the library. He without saying much came with me. We together entered that library once again. I was trying to bring back our memories. The library was not like before. It was all clean. We then sat on a bench and started to talk about the days after the camp. Then, after our conversations I took the cassettes from my bag and showed it to him. He asked, " Cassettes?".

I narrated the whole things to him. He became curious and asked me many things related to that. Then, it occurred to me about that portrait, I got from that room. I gave that to him. He looked at it, gazed at them and continued looking at the portrait without blinking his eyes. Then he looked at me in surprise and told me that, " I have something for you, take those cassettes and come with me".

I was just confused, but I went with him, since we were so close, I don't have to think about anything else. I followed him.

We reached at his home. He asked me to get in. After some casual talks with his family, we went upstairs. His eyes and lips were shining with happiness.

"Come, suit yourself, let me show you something", he said.

I waited for him eagerly. He then, came with an album and directed it towards me. We two sat on the floor and opened it.

Him: " Do you know who this is?"

Me: "Well, I think I do know".

Him: "He is the same one from the portrait!"

Me: "Oh God, yes it's him, they do looks similar, but...?"

Him: "I know what you're thinking right now".

Me: "Wait, this.. this is my grandma, how come?"

Him: "He's my grandpa and she's your grandma..."

Me: " So, were..they in love?"

Him: "Yes, of course, they were so in love that even the world was so envious to make them together!"

Me: "So, do you know their story.."

Him: "Yes, I do know".

Me: "How?".

Him: "My grandpa used to tell his stories when I was a kid, at first it was just a story, but, only now I was able to found a soul in his stories".

Me: "You're so lucky, I don't even have any idea about my grandma's life".

Him: "Hey, you don't have to worry, see who is here... I will narrate you their whole story".

Me: " Ok then, I'm all ears".

We then got away from his house. Decided to hear the whole story at that library. That library was like our meeting place. Our home, i'd would love to call it as. On our way back, we talked about our grandparents. We were so immersed in the miraculous fate. If I haven't met him, i'll never be able to witness the love story of my grandma. He had some other cassettes like I had, he had recorded while his grandpa narrated his story.

Chapter 10

A New Old Love Story
Story of grandpa & ma.

It was the time when most of the souls were filled with Cummings kind of love, but never understood,

"I carry your heart with me (I carry it in my heart)

I am never without it (anywhere

I go you go, my dear; and whatever is done by only me is your doing, my darling)

I fear no fate (for you are my fate, my sweet)

I want no world (for beautiful you are my world, my true)

and it's you are whatever a moon has always meant..."

(E.E Cummings, I carry your heart with me).

Most of the loving souls at that time was deeply enchanted by the words of romantic poems and novels. When the whole world was praising Shelley and Keats and so forth, we found the exceptional, the unconditional and eternal kind of love in Cummings words. While the world praised Shelley and others, I praised Cummings. For I saw myself in him. And I searched for a companion to adore his words together. Like Cummings, I too wanted to carry the weight of a heart in my heart. Then, we met. I saw my soulmate. When I saw her, I thought to carry her heart with me. She gave me a feeling that I should carry her within me. Then, I did it. I gave her a place in my heart. Every time, when I see her, my heart flipped double. My heart beated twice. "I want no world, for beautiful you are my world, my true" (E E Cummings, I Carry Your Heart With Me).

I whispered these lines, whenever I saw her. I always wanted and wished to whisper these words so loudly to her, I wanted the world to hear my love for her. I waited and waited for her arrival. I looked at her left eye, then at her lips and moved to her right eye. I tested the triangle theory of love. It never worked. But, I carried her in my heart, I carried her heart in my heart, like Cummings, for days, weeks, months and years.

One day, she came towards me and told,

"Saranghae.."

Eyes- filled with happiness, gave me an agreeing nod for me to carry her heart for the rest of the lives.

We fell in love. We agreed to share our hearts. She loved me like I loved her.

He took the cassettes out and put another one into the radio. I looked at him in surprise of hearing all these. This story had already made a soothing and enchanting influence upon me. The story got continued.

At that time, we were living at the same neighborhood, we became friends, then got progressed into close friends and then to 'lovers'. We were so in love, we were so in love with each other. No one knew about what we had in our minds. We decided to love, just loving will do. Then, too no one had knew or found anything about us. One day she called me to sit beside the river. She told me that it's too romantic and she wanted to witness it. I agreed. For I always wished to spend my time with her, those were the most valuable time of my life. We sat on the riverside, comforting ourselves down a tree. We two made sure that we are sitting with all the comforts of our body. We were just enjoying the beauty of nature and the art of river flowing without much pain. I kept my hands over her. Then, I took her hands to kiss. At that moment, I wanted to kiss her hands so badly. The nature was asking me to do so. But the humans weren't. Someone saw us sitting there and did the work of an enemy. Soon, and instantly her family left our neighborhood. Before leaving, she kept there on the riverside down the trees, something for me. A note and a radio. I took them to my room.

My life was so blank at that point. I became emotionless, having no idea of what to do next. But she had left there something for me to follow her. She didn't wanted to leave me alone. The note said,

" Write to me with your voice, your love, my darling.. I'll hear to them through the radio. There's a show where they read letters of the loving souls. Let's talk and listen each other daily through this radio. My love, I won't let anything or anyone to make us apart. For you had become a permanent tenant of my heart. For you my love, I had left this, I was forced to leave you, but my love won't leave!"

Then I started writing letters for her and sent those to the address of the radio station. We did it for many days and months and years. When the radio plays our letters, we recorded them and kept them secretly. No one will have a doubt towards us since the voice was different. We were loving so hardly, our love was so intense, that we were able to recognize each other with the words we used to write. We tried not to include the familial matters to avoid the problems that would arise later. Everything went smoothly. Her words were like having a hot black tea when it rains. It was so comforting. We wrote like everyday, about love, about us being together and many other things. How cruel the world is to make us apart. For the world is really unlucky to witness such a pure love. The world is envious, really envious. The souls that were meant to be together are pushed away. Where is love? Why the world including us are working against the beauty of love? We were helpless. Everything became a total mess, when her family decided to marry her off. I visited her family and asked them to give her to me, I ensured them that I will hold her forever. Their blind souls shut me and my love. They moved again. We lost our contact. I got drunked in loneliness. I don't know the rest of her story. For I was denied access to her life. I can't even look at her at a distance. They never even allowed me to just know that whether she is happy or not. I'll be okay if she's happy. But I know that she won't be that happy. This old man was then praying to the God to make my love happy. I hope that she should have been happy.

Chapter 11

Our Love

The story of grandpa and grandma is now over. We looked at each other. And was lost in thoughts. I gave him the cassettes that I had and he played. They weren't not long, but, what can I say, more than romantic. I sat there like I don't exist and I'm not hearing anything. I think that at that moment we two might have been thinking about the romantic skill of our grandparents. We were totally amazed. I laughed at myself for the romantic skill I possess. The day was almost facing its end. Why the days with him are always fast, I thought. I told him that I need to go home. We agreed to meet the very next day.

I became so happy and contented for completing the incomplete story of my grandma. They wanted to make it known to the world, but the world had played on them so hardly. So, they might need some help to make it known, to be discovered again. When it's done by their Grandchildren they'd be so happy in the heaven. It was my life's turning point, meeting him. His entrance into my life had changed me and my life a lot. The twenties which was a winter for a long time is no longer a frozen winter, it's beauty had begun to unfurl.

When there's you, the frozen winter becomes the beautiful garden.

The night was long, the world is now becoming envy of me. When the first sunlight marked it arrival, the old year made its good bye and a beautiful entrance was made by the new year. The village and cities were busy as a bee to welcome the new year. For me, the new year was already over with his arrival! I gave morning kisses to my mother and went to meet him at our usual place. He was there already, might be waiting for me.

The environment was so apt for a beautiful hug, but I had to deny them, they might be sad because of this.

"Good morning!", he said.

"Good morning", I greeted him back.

Then, we got together into the library, you know something, we are now close friends. I still think that there was nothing going by then in his mind. It was only me who had all the feelings. And I was hiding it well. For, I can't have a conclusion to what others feel.

We began our discussions, talked a lot about our grandparents.

He then vigorously turned towards giving me a shock and then he took my hands, stared into my eyes and said,

"Actually, if you hadn't come, I'll never have noticed this love that was kept hidden for long".

At first, I was enthralled, I thought that he was talking about me and my feelings.

"I had kept my grandpa's story till now, as an unnoticed one… Now, I know it's value."

He continued.

I sighed, "Oh God, I thought too much!".

I gave his grandpa's love letter to read. After that we went to the beachside and sat there on a bench. A stranger might confuse us as lovers. We do actually looks like a couple form outside. But, that's not the truth.

"And I'd choose you;
in a hundred lifetimes,
in a hundred worlds,
in any version of reality,
i'd find you and
i'd choose you",
said, Kiersten White in his poem, 'The Chaos of Stars'. These lines came directly into my heart and told me choose him over and over agin... Each and every words asked me to fall in love with him at each seconds, minutes and hours. They reminded me of him, and again reminded me to love him. I can't turn my deaf ears towards them, I was ready to do as they says.

We decided to take a walk, I wished to get his heart opened. The wind was on my direction, falling upon me, and was forcing me to be closer to him. The wind pushed me towards him. Then, I felt his warmth. I wished for the wind to last for more time, so that I'd be able to feel more of his warmth.

That day, I was so sad and depressed upon the thought of losing him. I didn't had any power left in me to tell him that I love him. The thought of him rejecting me itself was a fearful dream for me. I decided to confess my thoughts after gathering some courage. And I need to think of a way to confess to him. I thought a lot about it. How should I confess? Confession is not that simple. I need to think a lot about it, otherwise everything would be in vain. What if I gave him a cassette, after recording what I wishes for him to hear? That would be really sweet. Then, how should I give that to him. Hmm, I think, at first I need to prepare the things that I have to record... Ohh, how should i do it. I, then, laid upon my bed stretching my body all over.

I took a blank cassette and started recording as,

"How should I greet you, as a friend? Deep in my mind I always longs to greet you as my lover, my enchanting boyfriend. I know that this might be surprising for you, and I'm so happy to surprise you with my heart wide open. I don't know the reason for my love, the way it got planted in me, I'm still wondering. After you came into my life, it became so colourful. I'd love to call you as my life, will you give me a chance to name you as mine. My love for you won't get blurred, it's still growing! This lady, who wishes to be yours, is eagerly and patiently waiting for you to give me an answer."

After I was done with the recording, I played it, my cheeks were blushing. I covered the cassette with a beautiful paper and taped them with a beautiful washe tape.. I wrote his name and his address and kept them in my wooden box.

I was afraid to give him, as I feared rejection.

After some days,

We met again and talked about many things. We always had something to talk about. He have many admirers. Many girls have a crush on him. Every time, I find it impossible to take him as mine. I don't know whether I stand a chance in his life or not. I was always thinking about all these things, while we were talking. As before, we made the departure after some time of having long conversations. We met regularly. I got many chances to know more about him. We were now more than a close friend, a soulmate for each other. I could feel that, that slow process, of getting to know each other. And it's something, which was more than beautiful.

Chapter 12

A *Need for a Confession*
Want to confess:

Even though, I was happily enjoying the slow process of falling in love, I really wanted to be together with him. The most beautiful moments of love is the process of falling in love. I was totally enjoying it. Even after all this, I don't want to lose him at any cost. What if some other girls takes him away. I can't give them a chance to. So, I need to confess, confidently. I thought.

I still have that cassette I recorded in order to confess. But I won't use that. I want to confess my love to him, directly. It doesn't matter if I feel nervous, while confessing. This lady is not at all ready to lose him at any cost. I called him and asked him to have a meet up on the very next day. He agreed.

I was feeling nervous, but, I really wanted to confess to him. So I got myself tidied up and went. I wore a nice blue churidar with the bottom and shawl of same colour. Along with that, I wore a simple pearl ear ring, and had my thin diamond chain over my neck. My hair, I kept it loosed. I was able to see him at a large distance. His presence itself was an elixir for my eyes. I smiled so lovingly. As my steps got approached towards him, my heart began to beat, a rhythmic tunes, of love, they were singing about my love for him.

As soon as I reached nearby him, I ran towards him and hugged him tightly. I could feel the frozen posture of him. He must have got amazed. I hugged him for some more time... Soon, I saw his loveliest and the warmest hands approaching me. He hugged me back. I was able to convey what I felt in my mind to him with a hug. I trust that a hug for sure has such an amazing power. We hugged for a long. The world must have become envy of us by then. Then, I moved my eyes to him. And fixed my gaze towards him, upon his eyes. And I told,

" Saranghae".

I saw him smiling with his eyes, lips and his body. Soon we fell into a deep kiss. Don't worry, no one could see us.. Ha ha... We had entered the library, already before this.

Okay, now... we were kissing. His hands drew big stars upon my body. I ran away from out of shyness. He followed me and got hold of me and soon, we again, got into a deep kiss. He stopped it for a second and looked into my eyes and told,

"Nado saranghae".

He got back into the kiss. I could have made this confession earlier, I thought. That was a long miss, our lips were not ready to say goodbye. They became one. He grabbed my hands, and held them tightly. With each moments passing, the intensity was going up. I felt more like a blessed woman.

One of the precious moments of my life!

We got together. I got him as my boyfriend, so, now, I had done something that was impossible. God can change, what seems impossible to you as possible. My mind got pacified. He came into my life and made it, a sparkling one!

Later on, I gave him the cassette in which I recorded the things that I wished to say to him. We lived, a life of a dreamer.

"In your light I learn how to love. In your beauty, how to make poems. You dance inside my chest where no-one sees you, but sometimes I do, and that sight becomes this art."
(Rumi)
And I felt him!

Chapter 13

A *dream confession*

This part of confession is what I had always dreamed of. And, this is still my dream. Not happened, yet. You might wonder, but this is the truth. A plain confession is not what I want. For every words, that I use to talk about my feelings for him, I need to make him fall for it. So, I made him fall for me in the books. The confession part is what I made and it was included in my book. I wrote a book for him, a book that conveyed all my feelings. I tried to not to miss any of it. With all my efforts I did it perfectly. In my book, I included everything about me and him and my feelings for him, it had everything that came into my mind right after seeing him. I thought that by this way he would be able to see how I felt for him. The way I fell for him. It would make him understand that my love for him is not that simple.

I could even write the lengthiest book in the world, about you, me and our love. I hope to do. When I finished writing my book for him, I felt it, my love for him. It was all done by me, the printing, the binding and everything. I chose it, a different way. This kind of struggle is really enjoying, as all these are for my love. I wanted to tell him that I wrote the book and made it into a book all by myself. And that too for him, only for him.

The process of making this was something special, I felt so blessed to witness it. A whole book about him, my sunshine.

Oh my darling, i'm here for you, on my way to hold you and to name you as mine, wait for me, wait for this lady of yours, like the moon that waits eagerly and patiently for the night to come, for the sun to set. Let me come before you, to make you sparkle in my love for you!

With much happiness, loaded in my soul, I took my book and with a loving smile I walked for him, towards him. The world is so kind, for me to meet you, the world then became my friend, when they gave you to me, and the world became the precious one, when you and me became one. I held it, my book, so close to my heart. A precious thing it is, I protected it all cost. I knocked at the door of his, I knocked it again, again and again I did it. No one came there... When I asked a man over there, about him, he told me that they had moved away from this house and when asked, where?, he said that he doesn't know about that. I got fainted into the ground, crying aloud. I cried a lot that day. I despised myself for not confessing him earlier. And I despised me again for getting myself locked for many days without meeting him. I was doing all these to confess him by gifting a book about him and my love for him. No, I can't fail, I thought. But, I found no way to meet him. I walked to my home carrying the weight of my wailing heart and the dead soul.

I went upstairs and got into my bed and cried all my heart out. Unconsciously, I fell into a deep sleep. When I opened my eyes, it was already morning.

It was really painful for me to just have a thought of what had happened earlier. All my days became nights of tears. The snow stopped falling in me. The romantic fall of snow is no more. My mind turned into a desert, when he disappeared.

Between the flowers I felt like a princess, with my eyes flooded up with tears i thought what I would feel when you hold me within your arms, you were far away from me, out of my sight and out of my reach. Days without him, was filled with his memories. When I cried, I smiled in between when I recalled his smiling face. That face is still in me with all its freshness. I took my book, no, our book, and kept it close to me. I decided to look for him, when the night gets completed. And the night was over. I took myself out, to look for him. And my mind was tearing up because he went without saying me anything.

On my way, I saw us. They were having the best conversation! They were laughing. A fresh and calm air was there around them, I felt them. I had always wondered what it feels like to love someone, I was confused when I saw people crying out when someone they loves leaves them, now I knew. Your existence and smile and soul would be taken away by them, the only thing left would be your frozen body and sadness. While, there are some souls who finds their happy and calm soul back, even after their loved ones leaves them. I swear they are the strongest one in the world. Without love, this world is nothing. I found myself at the weakest point of life, when he left, but to get him back, I have to get my power back. For him, if I can't walk, i would crawl in the ground, nothing could stop me from reaching him. Today, the world had played a great fate upon us. When we were about to fall in love, when I chose to let him know my feelings, this world made us apart by distance, like it does every time. Then I realised that I should do more, so that this world won't even dare to touch our love. My mind was over filled with my love towards him, bitten by love, I was really broken.

Chapter 14

His departure

I realised how beautiful the world was when you were there with me, how beautifully my world had changed, how I changed into a sweet and smiling soul, I knew everything, and I felt them when you were left. My love for you was not that simple, I realised that too.

I'd say it loudly that when there is you, the frozen winter would becomes a beautiful garden, again and again and again. For your departure, made me a wailing stone, my love. Get back to me, I will be here for you, always... I chanted these like a mantra in my mind for many a times.

She went out in search of him, to find him, her love. For she carried his heart in her heart. The world became nothing, for he was her world, a beautiful world, like his Grandpa thought before. She carried Cummings kind of love. The past itself was getting repeated. While in the past, those loving souls were separated, while now in the present, she wasn't willing to separated, she can't let go of her love, getting away from him was similar to her getting collapsed... In the journey of no direction, she took a bus with no name, she went along with the direction that the bus took her. Her mind was completely lost in thoughts. Hairs danced in the air but they were comforting her by kissing her on those cheeks. The journey continued... And she was lost, completely.

Suddenly, a face appeared, a similar one. It took her glance. She looked back through the window. Saw there someone standing over there, she found him similar. When the bus had moved to some distance, the appearance of the person came into mind, rewinding in her like a movie.

That's him! Yes, I found him. She shouted. She got off from the bus and ran towards his direction. And she shouted his name... He never looked back nor answered her. She ran faster and hugged him from his back. And cried. That man turned around and asked, "Girl, who are you?"

That was not him. It was all just her feelings. Her world was full of him, so she saw him everywhere. She saw him even if he was not there. It was all just thoughts. Mind got cracked, the helpless situation, she was in, was really inexplicable. The world of lovers are really, a one to wonder! She felt like the world before her was about to crack, the amount of weight that she carried with her was beyond her capacity. She got herself up and went towards her home. Any words in English alphabets could be used to describe what she felt, but not as a whole. There are some things that we really can't explain or can't find any reason. And those things are really great.

When she reached her home, she shut the door, like a tight slap to the world for wearing a treacherous mask towards her. She wasn't able to find solace in anything. For she lost a part of her. You may wonder, why people are becoming depressed just because of a love, this can't be answered, but to be felt. Once you get this feeling, you will know the reason.

A pathetic situation it was. Even the tears were getting dried up. She stopped crying. But got buried deeply in her thoughts. He was not there, she had tried what ever she could do to find him. She thought and got afraid that their story too would end up like her grandma's. A knock, on the door. She didn't had that energy to open it. A knock again. She wasn't even thinking about opening them. A knock for the third time, she tried to get up and walked slowly. There was no knocking upon on the door or any voice. Then, too she went ahead and opened the door. At a small distance, she saw someone walking away wearing a black coat.

"Who are you?", she asked with a low and dull voice.

The wind blew over her face whispering that something good is about to happen, she left it unnoticed. That man turned to her side.

His face was not clear. She rubbed her eyes and looked at his face. The very next moment, the world witnessed her running towards that man with a happiest soul. On the way, she got confused if that was a mistake, just like before. She took a whole scan over him. And she found something, a bracelet, that was gifted by her.

"Yes, that's really him", she murmured happily to her inner mind and ran to him. And stood before him and stared at his eyes for some moments. Then, she asked,

"Where were you? Why you left me without a word?"

He gave her a hug, a tight one. And said,

"I am sorry"

She took his hands from her and asked him, "Have you ever considered me as your best friend?"

"Yes, why are you even asking me?", he replied.

"You could have atleast contacted me before leaving", she said.

"I had an emergerncy, it was my mistake, I am sorry, I won't do it again", he replied again.

She went inside her home without saying anything. He followed her. Then she came to him with a book in her hand, yes that one, she directed it towards his direction.

"A book! Is it for me?", he asked.

"Yes, its for you, take it with you."

"Oh, for me, okay, but why this book?"

"You may read this, the answer is there in this book", she replied.

Her eyes were by then filled with tears and her heart was beating and was asking her to go and hug him. She felt that weight upon her hands for not hugging him. When he appeared before her without notice, she became frozen, her feelings too. Deep inside, she was struggling to let her voice come out and her feelings too from the frozen state. That's the intensity of her love!

"As long as I have you besides me, nothing else could bother me", she whispered in her mind, the voice was so loud in her, only the minds that could love like her would be able to hear them.

A kind of peace was sown upon her. For she had found her solace in him. And he's back now. She gave that book, but she should do something from her part, she thought. That is, a formal confession should be done. What if he doesn't get what that book means. An ignition should be made from her part. A girl with no confidence was she before, but to pursue him, her love, she was ready to face them.

She always dreamed of them being together. A kind of love life, so calm, happy and a soulful moment would be it. Her love for him is just so pure, and she had made sure that it would never make him suffocate. A love should never be a suffocation.

He went to his home, with that book. He might read them. It would take some day. A lengthiest confession! And that too would be here in this world for many ages. Their love, them and their story would be known to everyone.

Chapter 15

A *Love Meet*

The very next day, the world witnessed something unusual, they met again.

Her: "Have you read the book?"

Him: "I read them!"

Her: "How many pages?"

Him: "I read each and every pages".

Her: "You read it completely over a night?"

Him: "Yes, do you think it as an impossible one".

Her: "I don't, but i'm really confused"

Him: "For what?"

Her: "It's just..."

Him: "Just..?"

Her: "What do you think about that book?"

Him: "That book, I really enjoyed reading it, a beautiful love story, I felt so lucky to witness such kind of a love story by reading them".

Her: "Oh, I got it".

Him: "What happened? Shouldn't you be happy for me reading it completely by a single night?"

Her: "Nothing, i'm contented for what you did".

He came closer and looked into her eyes and placed both of his hands upon her shoulders and asked,

"Do you have something to tell me?"

She raised her head up and stared at him and replied,

"I... I have...."

She wasn't able to complete them. Suddenly, she fell into a cry. She started to cry infront of him. And hugged him tightly. He stood in a wonder. She stopped crying and took his hands and held them tightly and,

she continued,

" I do really have something to tell you, I want to tell you at each seconds that I am falling for you, harder, again and again, I wanted to shout your name into the sky and label you as mine, I want to be yours, for you I wrote a book, to confess what I feel for you, I came there for you with that book, and you were gone, you know, at that time, I felt like I am dying with each passing moments. In this world, you were the only sweetest thing that had ever happened to me. I watched many others falling in love with the moon, but when I looked over there, I saw you... Let the world be envier of us, for the love that we holds. I want you to pursue me, to make me yours and to shout to the world that I am yours, label me as yours. You took all my worries away, when you kissed me on that night. You came into my life and lightened it, both me and my life", but he never heard them, since she could only shout all these inside her, because of the weight of stress she carried she became a numb. Looked at his eyes for once and ran away from him. He called her again, again and again, but she never stopped.

He followed her, but got failed to find her. At this moment, it was at this very moment that he started to think, about the book she wrote and gave him. He went to that library and read that book again. He found a very different meaning when he read it for the second time. Each and every words in them, was newer and fresher and were not like before it was. His eyes got filled up with tears, he read completely, he read that book... Now, he got, what she thought, her heart which was opened completely for him was known to him. He knew, at that very moment that she loves him. He closed the book and sat there for some time. He got fixed his vision to a farthest object. Stared at something, and was in melted in the deepest of thoughts. The moments he had with her came into him. Those moments which he had with her was left consciously behind by them. But, now it came back with all its strength. After some time, reality striked him. He stood up and ran towards her as fast as he could. On the way, he was worried that she would do something stupid.

He saw her sitting idle upon the hills beside her house. He ran towards her and sat there. She looked at him, and they both stared at each other. Even the nature was supporting their love, nature blew to them, a wind filled with love. While they did talked a lot through their eyes, that beholds many!

What happened to them? For you to know what happens next, let me give this book to him, the story would unfurl its own. He decides whether it's a happy ending or not.

Let me carry your heart in my heart, darling!

Dear,

Let me hold you, till this world takes

my breath away, let me love you and

name you as mine,

without you i'm just a rock,

my love for you would never
get faded away, it would
remain in me, forever,
with all its freshness. Love me
and let me love you, the world is waiting for
us to unite!

Chapter 16

H *ear me*

Things I want to Say Out Loud.

You're treasured and loved by many hearts, I am aware of
that.
But i'm not one among them,
look at me, with a special eye, then, devour my love with a
soul that's
unknown to others. Hear me with all your ears, my love
for you is not
like you think. I want to treasure you and love you and
care for you
by living with you. Feel me with a special heart, open your
heart and
alma for me, then, I will show you mine as well. Don't let
my love
idle, for me, you are the only world. Without you, I have
no world and
an existence. When there's you, the frozen winter
becomes a beautiful
garden. Will you be there with me? I want to call you as
'mine'.

Will be continued...

www.ingramcontent.com/pod-product-compliance
Lightning Source LLC
Chambersburg PA
CBHW031756150726

47989CB00006B/2751